BARGAIN WITH THE WATCHMAN

In Memory of Frances Klenett

EVA SALZMAN

Bargain with the Watchman

Oxford New York

OXFORD UNIVERSITY PRESS

1997

Oxford University Press, Great Clarendon Street, Oxford OX2 6DP

Oxford New York

Athens Auckland Bangkok Bogota Bombay Buenos Aires
Calcutta Cape Town Dar es Salaam Delhi Florence Hong Kong
Istanbul Karachi Kuala Lumpur Madras Madrid Melbourne
Mexico City Nairobi Paris Singapore Taipei Tokyo Toronto

and associated companies in
Berlin Ibadan

Oxford is a trade mark of Oxford University Press

First published in Oxford Poets
as an Oxford University Press paperback 1997

British Library Cataloguing in Publication Data
Data available

Library of Congress Cataloging in Publication Data
Salzman, Eva, 1960–
Bargain with the watchman/Eva Salzman.
p.   cm. —(Oxford poets)
I. Title.   II. Series.
PS3569.A46268B3   1997   811'.54—dc21   96–44441
ISBN 0-19-283257-3

1 3 5 7 9 10 8 6 4 2

Typset by Rowland Phototypesetting Limited
Printed in Hong Kong

ACKNOWLEDGEMENTS

Acknowledgements are due to the editors of the following publications in which some of these poems first appeared: *The Times Literary Supplement, Independent, Observer, Poetry Review, The North, European Judaism, New Yorker, Sibila* (Spain); and in the anthology *60 Women Poets*, ed. Linda France (Bloodaxe). 'Alex, Tiffany, Meg' won second prize in the National Poetry Competition of 1993.

Thanks also to the London Arts Board for a New Writers' Bursary 1996.

CONTENTS

BARGAIN WITH THE
WATCHMAN

Trepanned

Bad enough, not to have trekked the Himalayas
or smoked a pipe in the back of a Volkswagen bus
with Storm the mechanic, who, with blessings from us
changed the oil and filter en route to enlightenment.
Let's just say you were part of my dimmer days;
I turned the lights down low to cosmic bliss,
laughed at the spirit, in spirits, excited the men.
A corporeal slant. And all I wanted was this:

one little plastic piece of that five-and-dime belief,
a novelty axe to hack at the totems of numbers
on your PC screen. I wanted hand relief—
that is, the gentle touch just before you go under.
Nothing profound, nothing deep. Which is why
I let you drill that Black and Decker into my third eye.

Conditional

Given the edge of lilac
nudging the coolish air
—temporary, ripe for admiration—
given the circus of azalea
rounding off the lake
still pitch-black from a weight
of ice, or sheer forgetfulness,

every time, I'd take him in me,
an arrow forcing the point
in an uneasy truce, made for spring,
no angle left considered:
the calculated indecision
of this sort of love
that may be the only possible one.

Alex, Tiffany, Meg

rode fast convertibles, rose up like the Furies
blazing scarves and halters in a fire-trail.
The local boys, at first no more than curious,
went mad for the sting in their beautiful tails.

Such kindly girls; they deftly wound my hair
with strange accessories. Naked, like stone,
I bore the slender fingers and thundery stares
as they ripped and ripped away at my bikini-line.

Not ugly, nor evil, they were taken so seriously
their shadows slip beneath each lover, the fates
re-grouping nightly, featured in the crumpled sheets
or the legacy of silk, my abandoned freight.
Pursued or in pursuit, I find your street
and fly into your bed. Calm this fury, please.

Sexual Love

The motorboat's charge
trickles to shore, diminishing.
The bay tends back towards peace.

And that's why I like it;
though clamming by foot takes time,
a certain readjustment of the will.

At first, the mud's unwearable
for its soft give, the deepening
silent rip of ancient silk:

the way it clings around the ankles,
will never tear, or tears
repeatedly, the old healing.

Pilgrim

The beach was a shrine of steel in summer.
Its muscular heat stunned me face-down in prayer,

devotions buried in the scallop-shelled sand.
I was the shocked one, unable to faint

and impress the oak-smoked boys, the lavender girls
who just stepped over me with the meanest care.

How I kissed the shore of my shame and wishing!
And eternity rushed to meet them in a wave.

Night-Flower

He's drunk again, laid out on the promenade bench,
the sky-line's bright armada bearing down on him.

The river spins their early evening arguments
to smooth black silk. All the world loves a lover.

So a stranger now unzips that rousing dream of her
and in his mouth grows the artificial bloom.

The Lover of Women

strolls out with her at the earliest hint of spring
for a replacement hook: brass, Victorian,
just so. A lacquered grail to hang things on.
The one is not the many, the many not the one.
A lover of men, she follows, on condition
he feeds her those fables of some lout's washing
laid as gifts for a grateful wife. A sermon
the weight if not the worth of bullion.

Here's an abusive turn: he opens the glass doors
so that his companion may step lightly in
to a Versailles hall of mirrors, sinks and vinyl floors.
He adores labouring under a lady boss.
So why, why does he prefer an air mail toss
to the reciprocal warmth of his lover's skin?

Apocrypha

For Ann

We know how hard it is to tell the difference:
to tell if she had not raised her hands in amazed joy
but was standard-bearer for a dangerous river, her life,

snared by the warm wine and the shock of cold current,
a shoe lost, her foothold loosened from the velvet rocks
and long hair stretching like seaweed, from coast to coast.

How to tell? Hands had already erased the shoulders,
her wrist sacrificed to a tongue, one breath unwinding
when the tiny latch in her lungs had slipped with a name.

You could trace it back to a galaxy of her tears
—more empty space than matter, except from a distance.
Now to accelerate she hurls out arms, pedals into the dark.

It has long been our custom to disappear in this way,
with a careless spirit, the cables slackened then cut.
A spare thanks to saviours who leave icons on the shore.

Spells

A curse on the lover with shyness as a plausible cover for his
      black lies.
A curse on his leather furniture sticking to the skin.
A curse on his row after row of tasteful jazz
and the glass table's cutting edges.

A blessing on my cobalt blue vase
and a spray of lemon fuchsia, and forgetting.

A curse on 4 a.m., the light like soot or burnt milk in a pan.
A blessing on the dawn and dusk, when the sun and moon both are
      large and shimmering.

A curse on the memories like storm clouds in my heart.
A blessing on the storm clouds outside my window.
A curse on the useless letters I never throw away.
A blessing on my right arm for its sharp delivery.
A curse on my sharp tongue for its sharp delivery.

A blessing on the Lyric muse when she is kind to me.
A curse on the Lyric muse, for she is on holiday in the Bahamas.
A blessing on the warm salt seas for their constancy and power.
A curse on the razor-clams which slice bare feet.

A blessing on foreign countries: their birds and trees, their people,
      their clothing, their houses and songs.
A curse on their wars, our wars.
A blessing on their dawn, their dusk, their seas, even their deceitful
      men.
A blessing.
A blessing.

Tracy Pentecost

Sorry, but her folder is a disaster zone
with its alphabet of weak trees
uprooted in storms, left to rot.
Her abacus scatters its buttons
like a flock of doves at gunshot.
And who set the science lab. on fire
I'd like to know? That girl's history
is one of utter confusion and terror.

She's blown it for the entire class.
Run a cursor down the rows
and watch them topple like ten-pins.
That's the only language she knows,
and a million words in detention.
In one sense, anyway, she's fast.

Bargain with the Watchman

There were two extra hooks of a worrying nature.
You'd better say it. We didn't know what we were doing.

The cratered earth, woven with roots, admitted nothing:
only later, when the pegs slid in, the canvas grew taut.

We'd browsed along the Cantal roads like butterflies,
settling lightly in a peaceful upland spot.

But the dogs barked in advance of the enemy,
the farmer riding shotgun on his tractor.

I had to strike a bargain with the watchman:
ten francs, some unwanted perfume and a burgundy kiss.

My shadow's length weighed me down like a lover,
a nightmare pressing: rose-lit arches, confetti or skin.

I was clutching the drooping tail of a pale horse
while you tethered the body, secured the spine.

Useless, I memorised the army-knife's position.
Then we drank their flaming water. Vichy.

MASQUES

Can Clio do more than amuse?

I

Interlude

Thalia and Melpomene meet at The Queen's Head
by pure chance. Both dressed in second-hand suits,
they light each other's fat cigars. Then after,

they stagger home, strip off, pose on the bed
in a pantomime of woman/man pursuits.
Unable to make it, they dissolve in tears and laughter.

II

The Necessary Voyeur

There he is, the third party, the watcher,
the spare prick at the wedding,

leaning over the lit glass-case,
its exquisite illumination.

Urania had some errands to run
so the husband's minding the shop.

And does he mind? A glimpse of heaven,
flesh on the verdigris bedspread,

the lapis criss-cross rail of veins
on the lovers' hands, clutching

at the binary system he longs to break
with a stroke of his staff over the globe.

Are you Sirius? he makes her joke
while her lover's turning her over.

By the time the wife returns
he's carried away with Orion's belt,

her begging, begging him not to leave.
She needs him to do what she does.

III

Euterpe the Impostor

First there were commercial market forces,
marriage with a well-connected muse
and a formulaic kind of intercourse
aboard a tidy Caribbean cruise.

Then came the jerry-built song, a miracle
of engineering with a cooling anecdote
on scientific irony, unlyrical,
but lifted by an academic float.

Science parvenu! Pretender to the throne
by way of cosmically retentive slogans!
Your eau de parfum pheromones
and the blood like silken thread sewn on!

You! Atomic groupie! Undeserving
of the wife who takes you in your sleep unawares:
that handmaid spoiler—passion—serving her
invisible to you, consigned below stairs.

IV

The Male Polyhymnia Turns to Crime

Though his voice is enthralling, deep
as water pooled in a gorge,
with a timbre, warm
as bees, thrumming to the heat,

it simply isn't good enough.
He's jealous of his noble brother Calliope.

Why should he be doomed to harmony,
sotto voce, singing a supporting role,
penning sweet daffodil riffs for spinsters,
tired psalms, mumbled out of tune, low church?

He boils at a vision: the aproned helpmeet
serving condiments for the great chef.

A signature from Euterpe
on a calling card's mosaic of notes
earns a date with Clio.

A weekend's booked in Paris where
he plans to show her what he's made of, once
and for all, show her that he's not to be taken
lightly, or in vain.

V

The Hypochondriacal Muse

All that I am hangs by a thread tonight
—Anna Akhmatova

Clio's battery of tests yielded nothing
but a fin de siècle pain in the side.

All he can think of is hospital error.
He scratches his arm, then freezes in terror

at whatever he cannot make sense of:
scored tongue, the blood's ebbing tide,

sclerosis, cirrhosis—a boomerang synapse
and he's dead on target for total collapse,

hounded by symptoms he cannot control.
No wonder he cannot make love!

There *is* an unusual heat, lead in the pipes,
the body politic poisoned by clype.

Quick! To bed, for a generation
of so much diviner operations!

Euterpe longs to marry flesh with the soul,
while passion to him is a moment's reprisal,

a footnote, screened in the heart's tiny chancel.
Will needles in the groin make him whole?

VI

Terpsichore in Training

For guests I acted out my family part,
tripped lightly, mindful of her glass grisaille
lined up on the mantelpiece, a veritable city.
It reeked of formula: if I failed, she failed,
and this gave me the will to please if not the heart.
So I turned the empty gestures into something pretty,
risked sentiment with the deepest, darkest curtsy,
twisted into shape by her cash blackmail.

What a vastly overcomplicated debt!
I spot her zimmer, smile and mean it more
now the jewels are clouded, the bed is wet.
I surprise myself: an actress to the core.
We sip from the cracked bone-china tea-set.
The nurse hands me my shawl, shows me the door.

VII

Mneme as Salesman

In the basement of Allen's pre-fab, gnawed
by his dental braces, his index finger
inside me, stiff as a pencil
stuck in a sharpener

I switch channels to his mother upstairs
bobbing over dishes in the sink,
ignoring our Black Sabbath below, or just busy
rubbing with that cheap soap
she learns will never do the trick.

Meanwhile, Mr Etter is driving off to demonstrate
the Vacu-tron, the Slice-O-Matic, something stronger
as he sits on the edge of a hotel bed
gripping the woman's ears like handles.

VIII

The Muse of Spleen

May your lovers bite you hard and deep,
tattoo you with musical staves.
May they play cold whore to your knave
and then like schoolgirls sleep.

May they laugh at your jokes, burn the toast,
accidentally swallow the host.

May your potent songs astound
with their seduction leitmotiv.
May the silken scarves be beautifully bound
around your tactical brief.

May the girls all play their girlish role,
rule shyly, then boldly relinquish control.

May they take in their tiny hands
your swelling reputation.
May I use my tiny hands
in a different celebration

accompanied by this sexual psalm.
May the truth collect like rain in our palms.

IX

Possible Muses

Out back, out there

imprisoned by generous neighbours,
the only apron of earth I own
reveals a summer pattern

of blind fuchsia and blind snails.
I never iron, and what greenery lives
lives despite this stunning hand.

But let me tell you about the uninvited guests
for I set their place at table without fail.

Such a good custom for hosts
whose three graves are tucked in a corner
like border stitching:

one for me, one for my better self
and one for my lover, for you
who do not yet know who you are.

X

Terpsichore Twice

At Sousa's Music School on Baltic Street
they jabbed his fingers wrapped around a flute.
They made him kneel and fumble at the nest
of drums, or, seated, stumble over the piano keys
like upended coffins littering the open seas
where all the music of the world is put to rest.
When he broke a bone on the playground chute
they sacked him from the kindergarten fleet.

For what was he if he couldn't even dance?
A failure, no-hoper, who wouldn't stand a chance
but for these bodies made like instruments
carved from passion rather than good sense,
and since he could embrace this cello's girth
he played well, to pin me to the earth.

XI

Irish Lover

Erato's twin brother, dead at birth,
full-grown, with a hurley in his fist
left a ghost to field women's passion.

She weighs those hide-bound cork balls
in a matchless game which swells him proud.

Pinning row on row of butterflies,
he who deftly miscued towards the cushion
and struck off-centre to ignite her fire

is lying on his back, of two minds
about her loving his gentle power to withdraw.

XII

An Epic in Me

So that the telling may not be diverse from the fact
—Dante

Sweating, his body becomes hot wax
moulding me. I want my impression to last.

The weight of him is a team of horses
lumbering over a wooden bridge,

shoving, shoving on the advance guard.
Not quite bravery, but eloquent brawn.

He runs whole pitches through the night.
A hundred 'tries', he's no closer to goal.

Making his mark deep inside of me,
he stitches the laces of a cross, a dash—

he who loathes the intellectual.
With him I felt sublimely wordless. Until this.

POOR RELATIONS

Lucky Strikes

Her father was smoking fortune's cigarettes
in those gondola days. Golden boy. Teacher's pet.
Though he had far too many areas of expertise.
Chances are *he* found the morels, dismissed the lesser trees
she found beautiful, identified the tiny bird on the furthest
      branch.
Then there was the oyster ritual—the salt-water brooks
running into the sink, a childish lop-sided set of the mouth
as he jimmied a blunt knife into the weakest part of the hinge.

It changes, doesn't it; the chateauneuf becomes a binge
alone, at night, as he fingers the leaves of someone else's books
after the actress's brush-off, the failed business-lunch.
All his minuscule reputations will retire, migrate south
to homes in Florida, where the girls are less amazing, less
      amazed
and his bird-counts lengthen into the darkening glade.

Quogue Refuge

Only the sick can be caged
without a moral dilemma.
Yet here was a child's delight:
a hunched American eagle,
a dulled racoon,
the Barn Owl continuing to measure
the girth of our planet.

We had come once more to compass
the pond's perimeter.
We were the very charge in our circuit!
Horseflies butted the air.
The fields were rancid with milkweed.
Soon Maple Swamp would redden
its fluttering rags to a bull.

And did I not learn to love
the wildest things, out of habit,
dragging my adolescent weight,
impatient at Father Time
who never caught up with his binoculars?

There I stood,
bored at the back of beyond,
with a chance to break the set
and yet failing to twig,
having valued myself so long in imprisonment.

Boreal Owl

You could call it an outing, father-style:
driving the two night hours, hard on the single-white,
to that Connecticut wood, crowded already
with twitchers—the misguided, the obsessed.

Don't get me wrong. I like nature.
But I froze for ages slimmed behind
my chosen tree, the owl's fabled panoramic scan
failing to oblige the pencil-tickers.
When the head did turn, heavily indifferent,
he had to admit it was the common variety.
There were too many witnesses.
You can't complain. These are the risks.

Natural Habitats

A house for summer only, still its stubborn damp
outlasted August, sand lining the sheets;
though visitors practically rhymed their praises
over marasmius, boletus, cherrystone clams.

A panic of bees tucked itself into the eaves,
belonged, earning a season's grace. In the shade
father made himself busy with important papers,
his monster of a typewriter bucking and heaving.

Ace birder, he knighted himself with a nom de plume
—acres and acres to be overseen and written up by noon—
while mother spaced on shelves her rows of silenced jars:
the essential sugars of blueberries, beach-plums.

Snug in the hot berth of my bedroom, I cribbed for love
and studiously plucked my eyebrows into surprise—
candy and movie-magazines strewn across the covers.
They could never imagine what I was thinking of.

Double Crossing

For Jemima

They must have known that we escaped—if only
by some slight shade across their dreams—
how our cunningly angled steps bluffed the old staircase
from its customary whinge. Then, to be home free,

we'd only have to slow the screen-door's bite,
slipping into the crickets' deafening pitch
to take the first sprint through the pines which night
unified into something we'd hardly dare enter, but did

until we'd break through the boundary of parenthood
where the moon held itself over the marshes
patiently, unnoticed by us now released into noise
and racing down the beach towards the boys.

Grandmother

The bay's little waves licked the ankles
as her poled net loitered through the warm shallows,
seaweed caught and weeping from its bent rim.
Home again, ripples from the pail told the story.

When she rolled her trousers above her aged knees,
you knew where she was headed—across the milkweed field,
into the pines, past a single cactus and the oval frame
of massed catkins, to reach the wide open bay of pure joy.

Painting By Numbers

Now that the pursed orange kisses
of the trumpet-flower
have troubled the old walls enough,

the oak has broken the hammock twice,
the mushrooms have rearranged themselves
too many autumns in the same field,

something gives; tiny drops lightly sizzle
and a million leaves tremble and dip.

So I double-lock front and back,
wandering through each sandy room

—the hook-weave rugs damp and gritty,
the glass globes of insect cemeteries filling up—

to where the parlour's organ stops are frozen
in confusion: some Bach fugue
or just the whim of children.

Here hangs *his* version: our garage, but vineless,
young, its wide doors painted open

to a new Ford, a kerosene lamp lit
forty years back, before the haze
stole over his oils, distance blurred by trees,

before this thunder lolloping over
our pale and elemental house

crashes through the weatherboard
and finds me with the dog beneath the bed.

Anschluss

For Lorna and Eric

We summered in the lap of Peconic Creek,
one of the thousand warm cloisters in the bay.

Low tide slung out its most generous shore,
peppered with the breath-holes of softshell clams,

clumps of mussels knotted deep in the reeds.
But the neighbours opposite, in a smooth finesse,

deal themselves the acres we thought to own:
our marsh rewritten into the flawless sand

of Pine Neck, where new money grows gold potatoes
and folds the fields, like egg-white, into condominiums.

Their sleek pine dock has stilts, fresh as bread-sticks,
thin and snappable; chiffon floats out from motorboats.

We yaw in their wake, thumping the waves. An oar
divides the seaweed as we row hard, just to stay still.

Memorable

From the window of Mary's rancho house,
we could just take in the risk, the stillness
loading the summer resort, see down Fairline Drive's
repeating tic-tac-toe of x-marked glass
like hysterical fun, imagining Dune Road's docks
tilting all these years towards danger,
dreamy lobster boats bobbing at their tethered station
as the swell tries its force against the jetty.

But put aside the thought of dead and swollen animals
floating like bathtub toys, the weatherboard
ripped from country cottages, the flying cars
or the masterpiece of a newly-broken inlet;
that was 1937, impacted into your local guide,
someone else's thrill, a better tale, and true.

Poor Relations

1

This is your heart, a lump of quartz
with just a hint of amethyst.

Read the finished auction list.
Remove the Tokyo imports.

2

Your suffering is performance, and deserves a fee.
Let's open this Vaudeville nativity
in the upstate New York town of Bethlehem
(near to Auschwitz, Athens, Rome, Manoa)
where you agonised on a velvet ottoman,
ashamed of falsity—your feather boa,
your very genes of braided coral, the diadem,
You could have refused to go on!

Theatre modernised the witch's wand,
her gift of thirty-seven dollars banked
as standard rite of passage in the western world.
She spat in an elegant lacy handkerchief,
pinched your cheeks to rose, bleached you blonde
then had you waltzing for her prime antiques.
Most precious are these hardest words of thanks
to the woman who has costed all desire.

3

Free the floating souls from her paperweights.
Smash the Staffordshire lover's curls
and smash the strings on his muse's lyre.

Everywhere lies evidence—a missing limb
on the French rococo cherubim,
an empty place among the lapis horde.

Now behead the Celtic prince,
unmanned already without his sword.

Ah. This sounds authentic. A violent tryst.
There must be something in this
and in the curios like pearly hand-grenades
along the wall . . .

4

You told her how you *died* each tutu pasquinade.
St Vitus! St Genesius!
All the hollow-plaster saints!

Images in thrall
to the mirror's Aphrodite crest.

There were kisses like opals, crazed.
The kiss of her old age.

Which means you must forgive her all,
transpose each piece of wealth.

Applause like sleet
ticks on the wood of winter trees.
The lights go down. Finis.
You're feeling sorry for yourself.

This is the pencil scar
hallmarked in the palm of the hand—
the heraldic shield for the sisters of war.

If your sister couldn't dance, couldn't sing
and might as well have been nothing,
she'd take what jewels she could wear
to make the inheritance fair.

All women will be asked to stand
to be judged by diamonds and looks,
bodily wit and silver plate,
to prove how you're bound to reiterate
the greed and fury already long planned.

There are no true gods for these reference books,
only mortal indices of precious stones,
French paste, cut steel and mourning pieces,
stocks and bonds and sublet leases,
private schools, Art-Deco fans,
all picked up at bargain rates.

One Grand Tour each to the Holy Land
in search of more authentic roots.

When you measure your gloves against her boots,
the disputed satin gown—
which the servant ends up taking down—
you find you share a marbled spleen,
specially designed. You who thrive on loans
and privileges! The moths in wool
eating more, became less full.

Your sister is your enemy.
Each day you scythe through her memory
to clear the field for enmity.
So much for the golden age, this is the golden plan.

How to extricate the bitterness from jet
and tell the story from its artificial set.
Blood was a satin ribbon on the quilted bedding.
Here's rage drawn delicate in marquetry,
the milky vases with bisque flowers at their mouths
like petrified condolences
made more valuable as elements.
Someone's breath, captured in Venetian glass.
The blistered lemon bowl
was cut for geomancy
and not for punch or profiteroles.

The mind's in shot-gun wedding
with the object of its fancy
—no lack of ardour, be assured.
Now judge that stoneware's class!
Trash that imitation shepherd/shepherdess amour!

7

This has a religious cast,
his cock at half-mast
as he begins to arrange the scene in his head.
I'm reluctant to be naked on the bed.
Use it. *A convenient resistance.*
The bargain struck at his insistence.
It's good. Dark. Metaphysical. Am-Dram
has me squirming like the victim I really am
or intend to be.

> *Watch a woman come amazingly.*
> *Well-hung with his bronze artefact,*
> *he's done it. That last and best male task.*
> *Now he can relax.*

Surrender cannot be coerced,
though the broker's well-versed,
a stickler for technique and articulate wooing.

We both of us were salesmen, each with plans
but different currencies in hand.
Desire calculates its own undoing.

8

There is a jewel, Tiana Beach,
its agate pools just out of reach.

The sand across his skin
was buried when the tide came in.

His legs were bridges, strong and narrow.
I longed to lie beneath their shadow.

Blinding lustre! Then we lay down
on the forest's gold medallion.

The glory-hole was dripping glass.
Our island souvenir was cast.

Yet I never quite identified
the colour of his bedroom eyes.

The sand across his skin
was buried when the tide came in.

The fig-tree leaf was just a laugh.
I didn't know the joke by half.

The sand across his skin
was buried when the tide came in.

The moon played topaz tricks
in the form of an eclipse.

More fool me! That I reject
what was a genuine effect.

There must be catalogues, reserves
set at limits we deserve.

The sand across his skin
was buried when the tide came in.

9

Witness now the amateur's most obvious mistake
of lavishing an extra coat upon a masterpiece,
the so-called patient brush—heroic or discourteous.

Oh god, I am a fake!

I am gold in its most pure form,
too soft to hold a weight of fear.
Alloy is the answer here.

10

The satyr mustard-pot was never silver, the inkwell
never plate but worthless. So she sold them cheap.
Then of course they both change into platinum.
That was the luck a thousand charms dispelled.

11

You're the Queen of Misrule,
with a false pass through the fan-light portal
and into the penates vestibule

where Ethel, Gertrude, Ben are neatly hanging, so calm
and professional at playing mortal,
posed in the wedding or funeral stance.

Drink the sherry of melted carnival glass.
A toast to devalued heredity.
A wild dance.

12

Now that she's gone you can drink from Diogenes cup,
drink from those alabaster palms,
that priceless Art-Deco kitsch
always held clear of your childish grip.

Now that she's sound asleep
you find yourself loving imperfect items,
broken, unsaleably worn, of little worth:

washed-out jade, foxed ivory and horn,
old lamps with nothing to light them,

the astrological junk-heap
of Saturn's iron rings, a novelty Earth
disfigured with porcelain cysts,
outdated facsimile maps
and cosmetically altered angels, undone,
revealed in their true condition
—islands of amber glue on their wings
and fractured wrists—

as daylight splits the velvet gloom,
illuminating the family rooms.

The only things you can love
must be beyond repair.

The ceiling rose's plaster
is flaking grey snow in your hair,

the finials' dry husk of leaves firmly ground
to dust as soft as an old woman's skin.

13

The Queen of Misrule transmutes to an ass
on wheels, threadbare and rusty and browned,
jammed into the corner, unable to move,

as the numbers cascading from the face
of the backward grandmother clock,
faster and faster,
are swiftly, invariably replaced,
branded in from behind
like a Tiffany ornament signed.

You've shrunk, doll-size, to a miniature land
where *adorable* terrifies in the author's hands.

Air, water and grave.
What else can be saved

now you're tagged and buried in taffeta chaos
as the vaulting lurches and lowers,
closing your case.

Locked in! With only yourself to consider or break!
A decade of silence
containing the violence.
And just when you think it will never be over,
the cool air hits like a wave.

Somebody lifts you up by the neck,
hands you down.

Homesteading

It was official, in an American sort of way,
that the weather was obedient
as a dog on a leash
heeling close to each new settlement.

Ella Spawn was content for fourteen months
before she sold up for a cafe future in Williston.
Thereafter, Rush Blankenship takes up her written tale:
a line or two of marriage, and retail stock.
Beecher Leach of North Dakota,
remaining unmarried his entire life,
is yet remembered by some for his fried bread doughs.

See the bladeless windmill
stubbornly at attention in the hot wind
near cottonwoods ringing an empty space,
the corral's modernist geometry of sinking lines.

The buffalo wealth up the chimney for good,
now it's buffalo westerns keep you warm.

There in the central plains, one Dr Vernon
(later kicked upstairs into government)
crossed his pale white arm
over thousands of square miles, in a flash,
pronouncing them fair: *Rain follows the plow*.
The cloth got pulled out once the tables were set.

What of Thorstien Odden with his Hardanger violin?
What of Gilbert Funkhouser, that jokester?
Wherefore Stella Swab and Oliver Fedge?

Still, some choked on meat,
or ditched the prairies for the North or East,
anywhere of a greener or colder complexion.

Well. No damper in your stove pipe
is as good a fame as any, mark this,
or death in a flax bin,
or even a novel method of shocking the grain.

Victorine Berquist had the last word.
To visit neighbours, then up and walk away!
No sign to her shack she'd ever thought to leave.
No sign of her was ever found.
Just a whole continent, big as this paragraph.

Christmas at the In-Laws

The photos showed how they were bored: frozen poses
denoting pleasure in the garden, unholy alliances
forged, one midsummer night, without love.

Inside the reproduction home, they bent over backwards
on neo-Georgian furniture, memorised the statuary,
the brass fittings and sideboard's inner illumination,

every cancellation of surface: the dangerous glass.
Deftly inarticulate, they didn't admit her father was gone
until they opened the serving-hatch and all peered through

to see him passed out drunk on the dining-room floor
beneath the rosewood-effect hostess trolley
and a giant painting of thundering breakers

and then she always had to swerve around his empty place
wherever, as if to carefully avoid a porcelain figurine,
a limited edition so rare it had ceased to be visible.

Case History

Five-years-old, backed against a wall
shielding spring from L'Ecole Rousseau
and the paved yard endured at recess,
she's a wooden Babushka, painted shut
in a hail of stones. And who can say
that tiniest doll, the deepest version
weighty as lead, wasn't born fully-formed?

Children loop and veer, their after-images
tangled in furious games of tag,
the knot they tied still tightening.
Or were they her friends, just one bully
ferried to France and handed his rock
by a future grievance? (A further unwinding
would even reveal the doctor at her birth
delivering her with inauthentic love.)

So. Next door, she orchestrates maypoles
fountaining ribbons, a view of harmonious
pastelled girls, whose luck runs in circles,
the sundial leaning towards the golden hour
as they float inside, invisibly cued.
The tears are drawn to remind, not soothe.
It may *not* have happened like this. It's possible.

Whiteout

If I hold my breath, nothing will fray or melt.
If I hold my breath and rehearse my surrender to stillness

and learn how to smother these curses in white,
I'll hear how the ice breaks off from the soul,
the course of blood turned to water, neat, on the rocks.

Why should I be in love with such dazzling sadness,
the heave of snow right up to the black-coal river
roaming, like a fragile seam through the hills?

The town's jeeps are draped in satin, ruffles bloated
and dragging: the topiary of opulent cradles.

Now. The pendulum swings, after a frozen decade,
cracks the dizzying light. Someone finds purpose
—imagine!—starts patiently scraping, scraping away.

The future kick-starts, ploughs Main Street.
I'm free to go, now freedom has me by the throat.

Grief

I recognise those two full bottles, shared from hand
to hand, relieved of Campari or Martini Rosso
and tipping out a frothy wickedness I had forgot,
the summer light stretched to breaking point
across the park. At their age, it's work to drink like that.

Loiterers beneath a Victorian clock stuck at noon,
the eldest craves a more demanding role—
O j'ai mal à la tête. Je me sens malade—
one of elegant degradation; if he only knew how.

Odd, how blonde they are, as if from the same gene-pool:
the final drop of darkness emptied out, from all eight
of those naughty children, cool sentinels, the impostors.

Ursi's Arcadia

The bluebells had greyed,
the foxgloves waiting in the future,
the bracken ascendant in the pause between colour.

Prettiest from this angle:
Walter's thick oak, sideways now
and buttressed with fresh timber to mark his room

in their scowled paddock,
among the exhausted fallen-in seams
from which a Roman mined his life or death.

The sheep shouldn't complain
being sheared; they never know
they'll be lightened in this heat. An hour to catch them.

She couldn't help or hinder
the flowery tide which surged to the gate,
the unfailing yellow stars of the potentillas,

or the climbers sewing her in.
The row of marriage beeches had reached their extreme.
Allow her a modest folly: a Swiss barn—cross-beamed,
    red-wheeled—

the forest painted inside
so her mournful donkeys could look beyond their winter.
She said: This is the one creative thing I've done in my life.

OXFORD POETS

Fleur Adcock
Moniza Alvi
Joseph Brodsky
Basil Bunting
Tessa Rose Chester
Daniela Crăsnaru
Michael Donaghy
Keith Douglas
D. J. Enright
Roy Fisher
Ida Affleck Graves
Ivor Gurney
David Harsent
Gwen Harwood
Anthony Hecht
Zbigniew Herbert
Tobias Hill
Thomas Kinsella
Brad Leithauser
Derek Mahon
Jamie McKendrick

Sean O'Brien
Alice Oswald
Peter Porter
Craig Raine
Zsuzsa Rakovszky
Christopher Reid
Stephen Romer
Eva Salzman
Carole Satyamurti
Peter Scupham
Jo Shapcott
Penelope Shuttle
Goran Simić
Anne Stevenson
George Szirtes
Grete Tartler
Edward Thomas
Charles Tomlinson
Marina Tsvetaeva
Chris Wallace-Crabbe
Hugo Williams